Life in the Keystone State

Dennis Wolfe

Schiffer Publishing Ltd

4880 Lower Valley Road • Atglen, PA 19310

Other Schiffer Books by Dennis Wolfe:
Small Town Pennsylvania, 978-0-7643-4176-2, $34.99

Other Schiffer Books on Related Subjects:
Bucks County, Pennsylvania, 978-0-7643-4025-3, $29.99

Library of Congress Control Number: 2013946380

Cover Design: Bruce Waters
Type set in New Baskerville BT

ISBN: 978-0-7643-4354-4
Printed in China

Published by Schiffer Publishing, Ltd.
4880 Lower Valley Road
Atglen, PA 19310
Phone: (610) 593-1777; Fax: (610) 593-2002
E-mail: Info@schifferbooks.com

For our complete selection of fine books on this and related subjects, please visit our website at www.schifferbooks.com. You may also write for a free catalog.

This book may be purchased from the publisher. Please try your bookstore first.

We are always looking for people to write books on new and related subjects. If you have an idea for a book, please contact us at proposals@schifferbooks.com.

Schiffer Publishing's titles are available at special discounts for bulk purchases for sales promotions or premiums. Special editions, including personalized covers, corporate imprints, and excerpts can be created in large quantities for special needs. For more information, contact the publisher.

Contents

Acknowledgments

Heartfelt thanks go to the following, for their on-going enthusiasm, support, and encouragement:

> Charlotte and Chuck Allwein, Mt. Gretna; Bob and Nancy Bogar, McClure; Greg Capoccioni, Harrison City; Dawn Christ, Middletown; Linda Covilli, St. Charles, Missouri; Cos Curry, Berwick; Nebbie DiAugustine, Berwick; Amy and Mike Donghia, Linesville; Bo and Joan Fasold, Selinsgrove; Joe and Kathleen Herb, Selinsgrove; Jay, John, and Sally Hilsher, South Williamsport; Susan Hoyt, Huntington Mills; Logan Hulstine, Middletown; Peggy Hunter, Middletown; Wendy Royal and Marty Wilcox, of *Where and When* magazine, Mt. Joy; Buzz and Polly Savidge, Selinsgrove; Brenda Shultz, Bloomsburg; Patricia Wolfe, Cape May, New Jersey; the staff at Columbia Montour AVTS; and my aunt, Jane Young, Selinsgrove, who has become one of my most enthusiastic book promoters.

Also, I give thanks to my mother, Grace Raker, who always supported me, no matter what the endeavor, and to the many teachers and professors, whose dedication and knowledge gave me the skills needed to tackle a project like this.

Foreword

Writing a book can be a humbling experience. Only when it's too late to make a correction, an error here or there seems to jump off the page. I learned that I apparently have a fascination with the following words, *ad nauseum* and seemingly *ad infinitum*, in *Small Town Pennsylvania* and will, thus, come close to avoiding them entirely in this book: beauty, beautiful, serene, serenity, tranquil, tranquility, oasis, oasis of serenity, oasis of tranquility, first rate, grand old, and possibly a few others. Also, my apologies to the good citizens of Evans City, for, in one of my descriptions, uprooting them from their long-standing location in Butler County and moving them, without their consent, to Lawrence County. (It helps to have a sense of humor about these things.)

In many ways, this book is a continuation of *Small Town Pennsylvania*, but, whereas that book was organized as if it were one long road trip, this one is organized by themes. Along with portraits of parades, special events, and scenes from everywhere throughout the Keystone State, included in this volume are profiles of five Pennsylvanians who have each, in some unique way, distinguished themselves. You will enjoy and appreciate the stories of Anne Beiler, the late George Leader, Steve Sheetz, Michael Smerconish, and Brady Wegener.

Since the book is basically a pictorial, the text accompanies the photos, not the other way around. I made no attempt to give a complete accounting for everything seen in these pages, but the goal is the same: If you see something here that makes you want to know more, or that instills in you a desire to see it for yourself, then that goal has been achieved.

Geographically speaking, Pennsylvania is not a big state, but it's big enough! Traveling to every corner of it, and doing so when time, weather, and subject matter are all cooperating simultaneously, can be very challenging. Every attempt was made to be as thorough and as fair to all parts of the state as possible. Once again, one of my hopes is that people in eastern Pennsylvania will get a better look at what's "out west" and people in western Pennsylvania will learn more about attractions "back east."

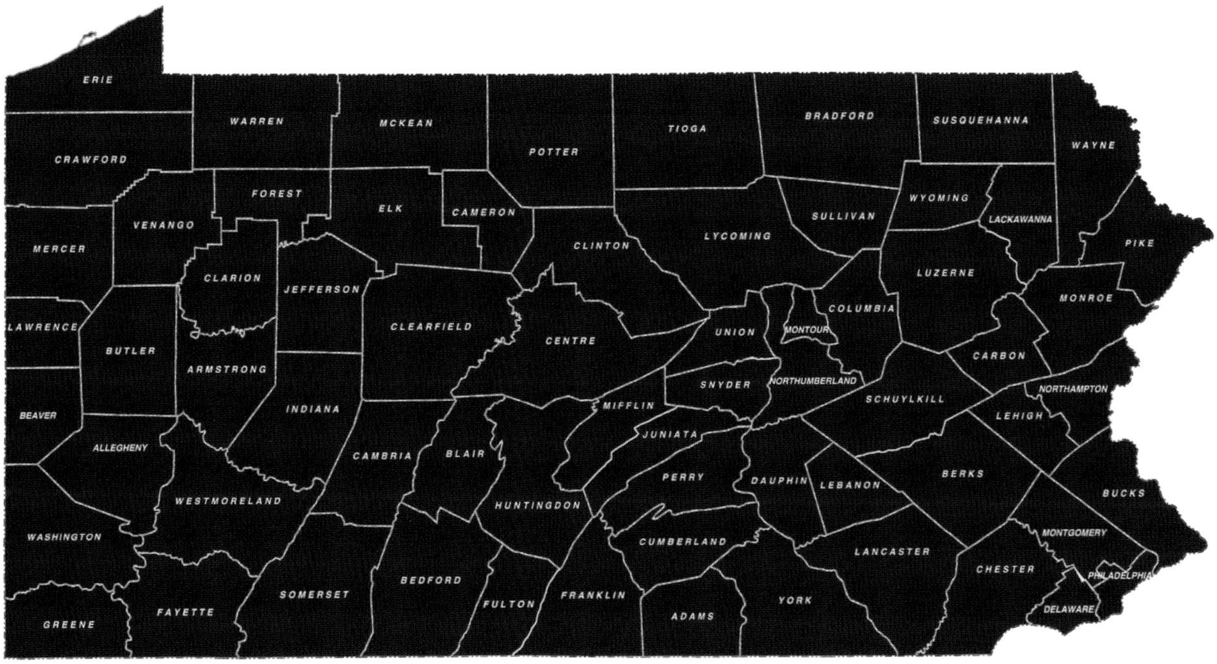

Courtesy of Wendy Royal.

The Ambler Theater, Montgomery County.

Chapter One:

Cinematic Treasures

They really are works of art. The movie houses that still stand are a nod to an earlier era, but they are also a reminder that there are some venues out there that are more interesting than some of the films they're showing. With the advent of malls, many movie theaters closed their doors for good, and most of those have been lost to history. The only way you could not enjoy these theaters (or theatres; I had to check the correct spelling for every one of these) is if you have absolutely no appreciation for art in any form.

The Campus Theatre, in Lewisburg, is an Art Deco masterpiece and has been showing first-run movies since 1941.

Designed by David Supowitz, a noted Philadelphia architect, the Campus, from front to back, is spectacular.

The recently renovated Strand Theater, in Zelienople, Butler County. I would have shown more of the exterior, but I shot this from across the street, and the roof of a parked minivan is about one millimeter below the bottom of this image.

The Bradford, located right downtown, is still going strong.

The Ritz, in Clearfield, shows first-run films and sports a dazzling marquee.

The Barrow-Civic Theatre, in downtown Franklin, has an active calendar of live and film productions.

The renovated and enlarged Dietrich Theater in downtown Tunkhannock …

You might be tempted to say that this looks like something you'd see in a mall. True, but it's an exceptional facility, and it's right downtown. Communities ten times the size of Tunkhannock would love to have something like this.

… Tributes to Hollywood abound here.

The Anthony Wayne, in Wayne, Delaware County. It's now a multiplex.

The classy entrance to the Bryn Mawr Film Institute, in Bryn Mawr, Montgomery County.

The restored Victoria Theatre in Blossburg, Tioga County.

To appreciate this theatre, you need to know just how small Blossburg is.

It's a huge asset to this small town.

The Capitol Theater in Milton is gone, but it lives on in this recently completed mural, where the building once stood.

The Circle Drive-In, in Dickson City, Lackawanna County, pulls in moviegoers driving along business US 6.

The State Theatre, in Uniontown, Fayette County, is a spacious facility.

The outer lobby …

… The inner lobby …

… The theatre's main seating area.

Annville, in Lebanon County, is home to the Allen Theatre.

Part of the package at the Allen Theatre is the adjoining coffee house.

This Art Deco structure houses the County Theater in Doylestown, Bucks County.

A movie so bad, the audience runs from the theater! Actually, this is part of Blobfest, an annual event in Phoenixville that re-enacts a short, but famous, scene from the 1950s movie *The Blob*, which starred Steve McQueen and Aneta Corsaut (Helen in the *Andy Griffith Show*). The marquee is exactly as it was in the film.

It wasn't there a few minutes ago, but now it is — The Blob!

Clouds are part of the sky in Carmichaels, Greene County.

The Guthrie Theatre in Grove City.

The Roxy Theatre, in downtown Northampton, gets your attention with its brilliant marquee!

The very hospitable owner for more than forty years, Rick Wolfe (no relation), was eager to show me the theatre's interior, which is a repository of Art Deco design.

The theatre was designed by David Supowitz, the same architect responsible for the Campus Theatre in Lewisburg.

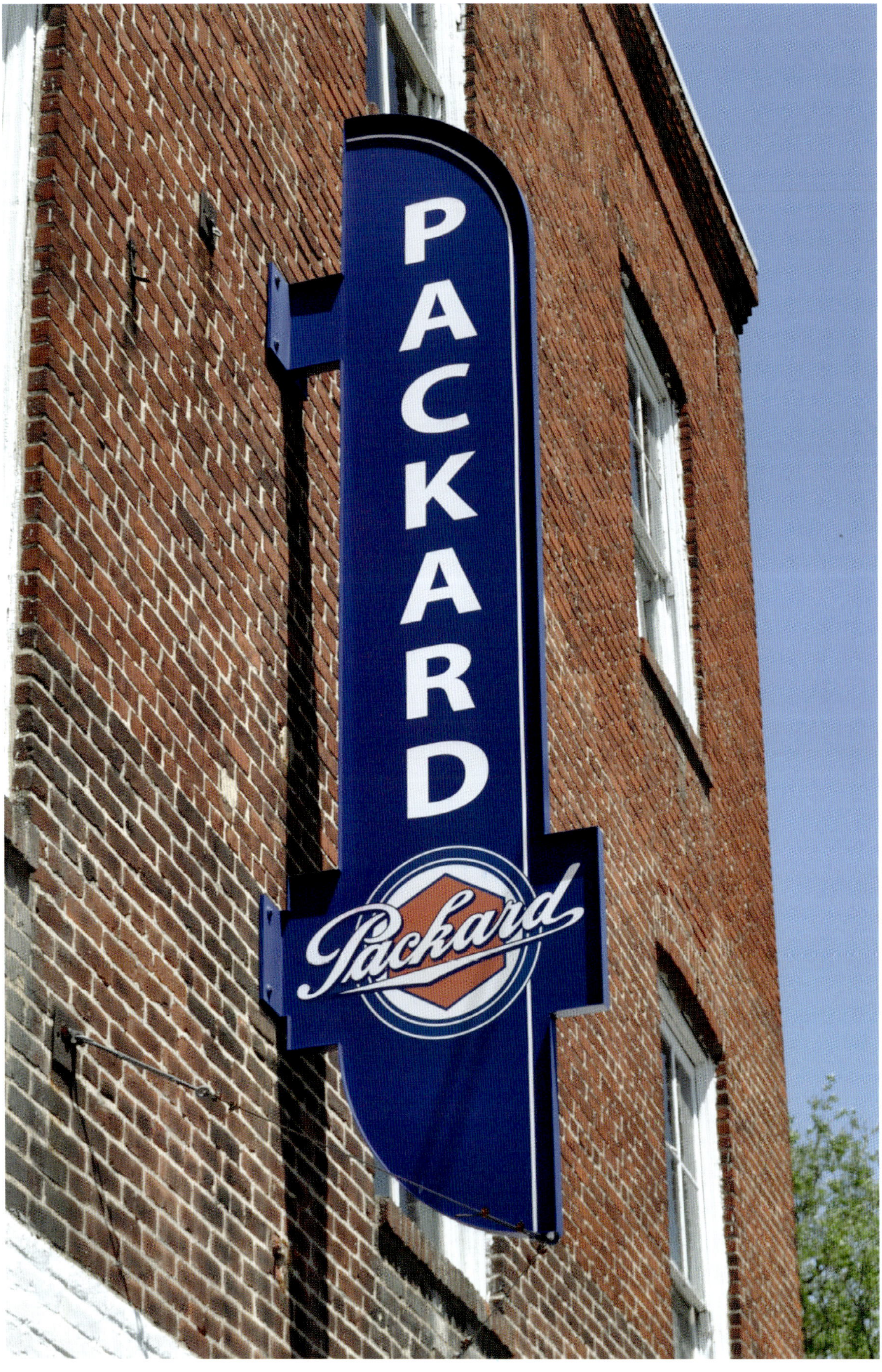

This sign in Shenandoah, Schuylkill County, was here when new Packards were still for sale! It has only been taken down for painting.

Chapter Two:

Planes, Trains, and Automobiles

Car shows are found all over the state. Some are huge, some quite small, but all of them display the appeal of classic vehicles, and the dedication of their owners in maintaining them.

Train excursions, from the Strasburg Railroad chugging its way through picturesque Amish country in Lancaster County, to the Oil Creek and Titusville Railroad exploring the heritage of the Oil Creek Valley, still have a mystique that riders young and old enjoy.

Air shows are an exhibition of raw courage of daredevil pilots who get thrills just from being able to entertain eager onlookers.

A Ford Maverick in Newtown, Bucks County.

This classic 1950s Studebaker sparkles on Seneca Street, in Oil City.

An AMC Rambler in Macungie, Lehigh County.

A Camaro in Marysville, Perry County.

Is that an inquisitive youngster looking over this vintage Ford in Hawley, Wayne County? No, he's not real.

A 1952 Oldsmobile in Sharon. It's a beautiful car, but the combination of the hood ornamentation and the grill reminds me of a catfish.

A Corvette at the outstanding Beaver Falls Car Cruise, held in mid-June.

"GR-RRR!" in Newtown.

A 1955 Chevy in Newtown, complete with "car service."

Don't try to eat any of this (it isn't real), but the display does evoke some fond memories.

This 1923 Ford, in Revloc, Cambria County, *may have been* altered slightly since it was built.

If it's an Edsel, you have to highlight the grille, I suppose, but really, I did so because the car was parallel parked in Ligonier, and this was as far away as I could get from it!

Downtown Bloomsburg is the scene for this Mercury Cougar.

In Middletown, Dauphin County, there's a stray dog about to — no, wait — it's just a prop!

OK, I won't! (This "advice" comes to you from Arch Street, in Sunbury.)

Mustangs one and two at the Ambler car show.

Also in Ambler, here's this interesting contraption: a 2002 Corbin Sparrow.

In honor of the Pocono Raceway Festival, in downtown Stroudsburg.

Gene Burd, with some advice from his dad, gets ready to take the track at Selinsgrove Raceway Park.

This shot, taken at the Blossburg State Coal Festival, is a nice introduction to . . .

. . . this one, where Morgan Lawton stands by her Jeep in Espy, Columbia County.

Back in Oil City, the crowd waits to see some burning rubber — and they get some burning rubber.

Near Benton, Columbia County, just some good ole boys, never meanin' no harm. John Miller and brothers Mike and Vaughn stand by their 1983 Chevy truck, a work in progress.

Returning to Macungie, we're back in the 1920s, and Calvin Coolidge did win the election, in case you were wondering.

It's Harley time in Cross Fork, Potter County.

This is just part of an impressive train layout put together by the Milton Model Railroad Club. A replica of downtown Milton, it's faithful in almost every detail.

Another major layout is on display by the Lewistown Model Railroaders Club.

Members of the Lower Anthracite Model Railroad Club, in Shamokin, maintain this outstanding display, open on numerous occasions around Christmas.

"All aboard" … for the Christmas excursion in Bellefonte.

A fully-restored trolley at the Rockhill Trolley Museum in Huntingdon County.

The very popular Thomas the Tank Engine occasionally visits the East Broad Top Railroad in Orbisonia, literally just across the street from Rockhill.

Maybe the Great Northern Railroad never made it to Erie County, but this dining car in North East can be explored at the Lake Shore Railroad Museum.

Among tractor lovers, there's as much of a rivalry between the various makes as there is between Ford and Chevy lovers. Here's a vintage John Deere in Troy, Bradford County.

An International Harvester in Shirleysburg, Huntingdon County.

A New Holland at the Manheim Farm Show in Lancaster County.

At the Lock Haven Fly-In, you certainly can expect to see Piper Cubs, which were manufactured on this very site.

Where there's a Piper, there's a cub!

This visitor to the Fly-In is a Douglas C-54, and was one of the planes used to haul cargo during the Berlin Airlift of 1948-49. History that gives you chills!

The Air Heritage Museum in Chippewa, Beaver County, is also a repair and rebuilding facility.

The Penn Valley Airport in Selinsgrove plays host to this thrilling air show.

Back in Lock Haven, some real speed!

National Gold Medal Winner

PA

State Parks

Best in the Nation

2009 - 2011

Every state has great state parks, but Pennsylvania's are among the best.

Chapter Three:
State Parks

Pennsylvania's state park system is consistently recognized for its excellence, and has the honor of being named best in the nation for 2009-2011 by the American Academy for Parks and Recreation. It was the goal of Maurice K. Goddard, secretary of what was then the Department of Forests and Waters, to ensure that there would be a state park within twenty-five miles of every resident of Pennsylvania, and he nearly succeeded. First appointed by Governor George Leader, Dr. Goddard was the lynchpin for making our state parks what they are today. They aren't just ecologically diverse sanctuaries; they also provide great opportunities for people to enjoy all of nature's offerings.

Just after sunrise on a cool morning in early summer, the Nature Inn at Bald Eagle State Park, Centre County, looks out over Foster J. Sayers Lake.

At the lake, the sounds of chirping birds, and the sight of about two million (more or less) rabbits, greet the early riser.

The Nature Inn is an eco-friendly hotel that is fairly new to the park. This facility is so "green" that even the curb stops in the parking lot are made of recycled plastic milk bottles.

The appropriately designed window is above the entrance to the dining room.

The countertop at the check-in desk is made from the crushed hulls of sunflower seeds!

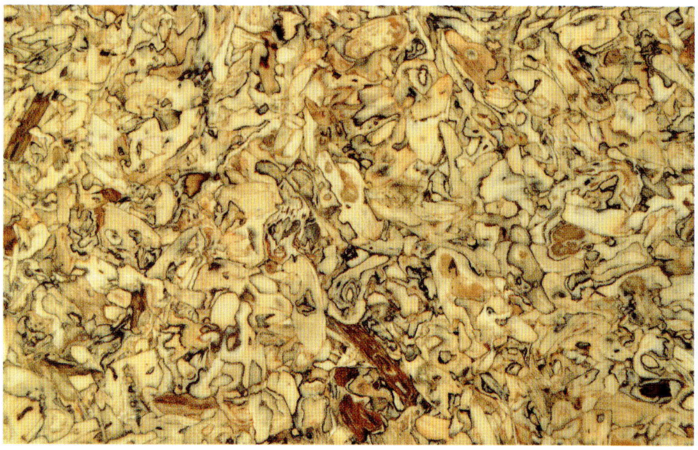

George M. Leader

Businessman, Former Governor, Humanitarian

He was humble, enduring, and a man of integrity. In short, he was amazing. George Leader was the governor of Pennsylvania from 1955 to 1959, and was only the second Democrat to be elected to that post since 1934. Describing himself as "just a chicken farmer," he took advantage of the values learned from his simple York County roots to advance causes that were important to him. As governor, he led the way for significant reform of the state's mental institutions and tried, with at least some success, to clean up the state's patronage system. He also appointed Dr. Maurice K. Goddard to head the Department of Forests and Waters, now the Department of Conservation and Natural Resources (DCNR). That appointment was one of Governor Leader's lasting legacies, as Dr. Goddard continued to hold that position through the administrations of several succeeding governors, enabling him to develop Pennsylvania's state park system into one of the country's best.

According to the state constitution then in effect, Governor Leader could not run for re-election and, once out of office, he never ran for another elected position. In the last few years of his life, looking at the more than fifty years that have passed since the end of his term, he expressed concern about what he called the fiscal irresponsibility of both political parties, especially over the past twenty years, leaving future generations holding the bills.

After his political life seemed to be finished, he began a career in what could best be described as providing facilities and opportunities to make life better for others. The Leader Family established the Country Meadows retirement facilities, and later, Providence Place, an assisted living facility with four locations, in Hazleton, Pottsville, Dover, and Chambersburg.

In his book *Challenging Complacency*, Kenneth C. Wolensky notes that a recurring theme in the governor's life was his positive nature and his satisfaction in giving to others. The governor did missionary work in Africa, which included programs to educate, feed, and clothe those in need. He was also involved in a prison ministry and a program to provide computers in less affluent schools. Just a few months before his passing, I asked him what kept him going in his mid-nineties, and he said that he loved what he was doing. I also asked him how he would like to be remembered, and, without hesitation, he answered "humanitarian." How could anyone disagree? George M. Leader, 1918-2013. What a remarkable Pennsylvanian.

George Leader, in his office in Hummelstown, next to the *Time* magazine cover photo from election night, 1954.

Water lilies can be found everywhere, but you're sure to see them by the hundreds at Black Moshannon State Park, in Centre County.

It's a spectacular flower!

Early morning at Canoe Creek, in Blair County, caught this bullfrog undecided as to its next move.

Chapman State Park, near Clarendon, Warren County, is the site of Winterfest, held in late January.

There wasn't much snow this time, but the dogs still got a run.

Food stands, just like it was summer.

Proof that you can have a good time in winter, too.

For its untouched stands of forest, and the winding Clarion River, Cook Forest State Park is one of Pennsylvania's "must see" state parks.

A blacksmithing demonstration during a French and Indian War re-enactment.

The cannon is real — and so is the noise!

Even in March, you shouldn't be surprised to see a coating of snow at Denton Hill, Potter County.

Maybe not-so-well-known outside of northeastern Pennsylvania, Frances Slocum State Park, near Dallas, Luzerne County, is great for a day away from the crowd.

The lake has better reflecting properties than a bowl full of mercury! (Don't mess with mercury — the water is safer!)

Boulder Field, in Hickory Run State Park, Carbon County, is a surprise to first-time visitors.

Fall colors in a mixed forest like this one complement the exceptional geology of this site …

... If a tree can take root, it will.

In total, Boulder Field covers more than sixteen acres.

In some areas of Hickory Run, *Kalmia latifolia*, the state flower, blooms in profusion, usually from early- to mid-June.

Mountain laurel is showy, collectively and individually.

Hyner View State Park, near Renovo, Clinton County, has one of the most panoramic views in Pennsylvania.

At various times during the year, there are hang-gliding events.

Air currents need to be just right …

… Finally, take-off is imminent.

An old Civilian Conservation Corps (CCC) dam from the 1930s still stands in Kettle Creek State Park, Clinton County.

Kinzua Bridge State Park, McKean County, preserves what's left of what was once the highest railroad bridge in the country.

A tornado ripped through the valley in 2003, knocking down much of the bridge.

At Lackawanna State Park, north of Scranton, the kayaks are in for the evening.

Only a few of our state parks have recreational facilities of this type. This one is in Little Buffalo State Park, Perry County.

This picturesque section of Slippery Rock Creek is found at McConnells Mill, Lawrence County.

Blackberries, in various stages of ripening, thrive in a section of Moraine State Park, Butler County.

It isn't the entrance to a state park, but the Quehanna Highway, shown at its northern terminus near Medix Run, Elk County, provides the same kind of wilderness experience.

Along that highway, the Marion Brooks Natural Area features a stand of white birch trees that is unusually large for Pennsylvania.

This disappointed pup isn't too pleased at being left behind while the family takes a dip in the Youghiogheny River at Ohiopyle State Park, one of Pennsylvania's biggest and best

This takes courage and skill. No, not getting the photo — plunging over the twenty-foot-high Ohiopyle Falls! DCNR allows this exhibition of bravado just once a year, in August.

Kids and adults alike took part in Ohiopyle's Winterfest activities, though it sure took these young ladies a long time to decide to go down that hill!

Just one of many scenes in the Ohiopyle town site: the exterior has been painted since this picture was taken, but the weather-beaten look here kind of adds character to the shot.

This rail trail is part of the Great Allegheny Passage, which is part of a continuous route from Pittsburgh to Washington, D.C. ... These two are riding for the benefit of the photographer. One can only hope they weren't planning to go the eleven miles to Connellsville on those bikes.

Cucumber Falls is classified as a bridalveil falls, for what should be obvious reasons,..

On the road leading to Cucumber Falls, you might be lucky enough to see White Trillium in late April.

Among the white ones can be found Purple Trillium, but in far fewer numbers.

The genus is *Russula*, and the species is possibly *emetic*; then again, it might be *xerampelina*. Mushroom identification can be tricky. Let's call it a red russula.

This is a blue flag, or, if you like, an iris.

See the previous russula for "positive identification." In this picture, though, the snail is an added attraction!

Amanita inaurata, under a canopy of trees, not far from where the Youghiogheny River passes under the high rail trail bridge.

A violet branched coral is proof that a fungus can be as eye-catching as any flower.

Cardinal flower. An easy one to identify!

Winter at Parker Dam, Clearfield County, is glorious.

The Salami Sling, is, well, a salami-throwing contest. It doesn't translate well into a still picture!

This is one of a number of Civilian Conservation Corps (CCC) buildings that can be found at Parker Dam. The original roof was blown off in a devastating 1985 tornado, but the sturdy walls remained intact.

Peg and Jim Beddall, of Selinsgrove, gaze at the eight hundred-foot-deep Pine Creek Gorge, also known as the Pennsylvania Grand Canyon, from Leonard Harrison State Park.

Leonard Harrison, on the east rim of Pine Creek Gorge, is a rewarding visit anytime of the year …

… Including the solitude you'll often find if you come here during the winter.

Mt. Pisgah State Park, Bradford County, is in the heart of the Northern Tier.

That lone iris in the previous picture? Here it is.

The Kellogg family, from nearby Troy, innocently enjoying a perfect Sunday afternoon, were kind enough to stop for this picture. The trail is so named as a reminder that this is Stephen Foster country.

It's just an opening in the woods, but quite an impressive one. R.B. Winter State Park, in western Union County, has lots to offer in the summer . . .

. . . and in the winter, too.

Kitchen Creek plunges over Ganoga Falls, the highest at Ricketts Glen State Park, in Luzerne and Sullivan Counties, plus a tiny sliver of Columbia County.

From the bottom, it may not seem that high, but, at ninety-four feet, it's impressive.

Fungus alert! This is a chipmunk's eye view of a chicken mushroom. The camera was set on the rocks and pointed upward, at the underside of this fungal growth.

It's the same mushroom, but taken with a flash. Note the loss of translucence, and the now high visibility of water droplets. The best part of this is its name. It is so called because (and I'm not making this up) it tastes like chicken. (But don't ever eat a mushroom unless you can positively identify it. If you get symptoms from eating a poisonous one, serious damage has already been done.)

Adams Falls is the last in a bunch of falls, and is the most accessible to the highway, just off PA 118.

Sheldon Reynolds Falls, near the bottom of the Glen.

Murray Reynolds Falls, the first on the Falls Trail, if you're going from bottom to top.

The falls aren't the only attraction. In springtime you're likely to see a family of geese on Lake Jean.

One of the joys and/or hazards of being a teacher is being recognized by current and former students almost wherever you go. Dakota Olson and Dakota Shultz happened to be in the right place at the right time for this picture.

When the water is warm enough, the lake is a magnet for sunbathers and swimmers.

This view, from the Shikellamy State Park Marina, looks across to the confluence of the west and north branches of the Susquehanna River, at Northumberland. The plaque shows a map of the complete Susquehanna River watershed, with the West Branch rising in northern Cambria County, and the North Branch beginning as an outlet of Lake Otsego, in Cooperstown, New York.

From the Shikellamy State Park overlook, across the way from the Marina, this standard view almost never fails to reward the visitor. The West Branch is at bottom, while the North Branch flows from the rising sun.

The previous picture was taken from the cliff on the left. It would be great to be able to say that both pictures were taken on the same day, but they weren't. In case there was any doubt, it is the same sun, though. (Sorry, it was just too easy.)

Sinnemahoning State Park, Cameron County, is located in one of the most remote areas of the state.

Early snow and late fall make a great contrast at Tobyhanna State Park, Wayne County.

Virginia Bluebells can be found in Tyler State Park in late April.

Located near Newtown, Tyler State Park is an island of calm in a heavily populated area of Bucks County.

It's 6:02 a.m., and there is no one else around, at Yellow Creek State Park, Indiana County. Savor the solitude.

This is one of six wood carvings that anchor each end of three benches in downtown St. Marys. It's part of a project to establish "woodlins" throughout Elk County.

Chapter Four:

Streetscapes and Openscapes

First of all, I'll admit to making up the word "openscapes," but it fits. These are scenes — downtown, uptown, and out of town — that are arranged mostly in alphabetical order.

A Scout project in Bangor, Northampton County.

Third Street is Beaver's main shopping street …

… It features numerous specialty shops like this bakery.

Preparation for a 1950s-style sock hop unfolds in Bellefonte, in this view from high atop the former Garman Opera House.

One of Bellefonte's many leafy neighborhoods.

The windows reflect a late evening sky in Bradford, McKean County County.

My guess is that they have it…somewhere.

California lies on a bend in the Monongahela, in this view looking south.

Lesser-known than Conneaut Lake, Canadohta Lake, in Crawford County, is just as appealing.

This certainly isn't the Susquehanna! This vessel is found on the Monongahela River, near Speers.

Michael Smerconish apparently is one of those people who has found a way to fit thirty hours of activity into a twenty-four-hour day. As you might expect, the native of Doylestown has an accomplished résumé. He writes a twice-weekly column for the *Philadelphia Inquirer*, hosted a nationally-syndicated daily radio show, and is frequently a guest and substitute host on MSNBC. Early in 2013, he moved to SiriusXM satellite radio. He has also authored five books, most of the proceeds of which have been donated to charity, and continues to be a member of the Pennsylvania Bar as an associate of the law firm of Kline and Specter.

While still in college, he was an advance man for Vice President George H. W. Bush and was appointed regional director for the Department of Housing and Urban Development. He is a graduate of Lehigh University and the University of Pennsylvania Law School.

Michael began his daily radio show in 2002 and was the first radio host to interview President Obama from the White House. Recognized as Philadelphia's best talk show host, and one of the city's most influential figures, he is most proud of hosting a program that is entertaining, but still maintains a decorum of civility. He has strong concerns that the negative national discourse is being set by talk radio and cable hosts, and he has worked hard to be a positive influence. He believes that those who disagree with him should be able to say that they may not like what he says, but are not offended by the manner in which he says it.

When I asked him how he would like to be perceived, his simple answer was: "Tolerant of all viewpoints."

Michael listens intently to a caller on his nationally-syndicated daily radio show, broadcast from WPHT studios in Bala Cynwyd, just across City Avenue (aka City Line Avenue) from Philadelphia …

… and now at his new gig with SiriusXM.

The reference is to a 1948 weather system that, for days, prevented the escape of pollutants from a factory, causing numerous deaths and thousands of illnesses. Because of this incident, efforts to curtail air pollution began to take on more urgency.

Potomac Avenue in Dormont looks deserted at the moment, but it's a thriving area in this borough just south of Pittsburgh.

The Bucks County courthouse is situated just north of downtown Doylestown.

This feast for the eyes is the Cambria County Courthouse in Ebensburg.

The mule's name is Emma, and it's in Emmaus, Lehigh County. The figure was constructed as a community project.

The main square in Elizabethtown, Lancaster County, is a great place to meet and relax.

On Liberty Street, in Franklin, you'll see this exterior, which should be enough to draw you inside for a huge collection of antique musical instruments.

Franklin knows how to put on special events. This is at Applefest®, an event so big that it even has its own "®".

Looking eastward from downtown Girard, Erie County.

The Schuylkill River flows out of the mountains in the north, past the town park in Hamburg, Berks County.

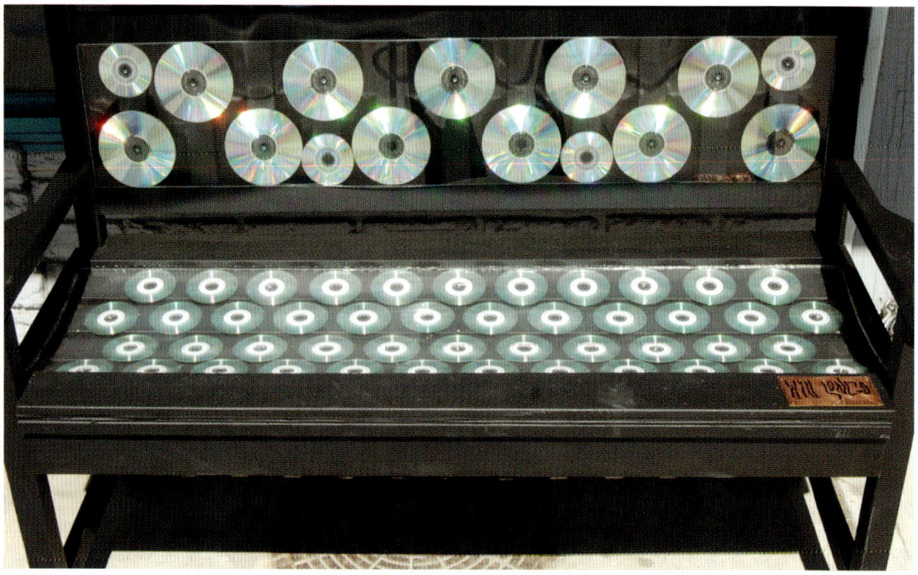

Do you play it or sit on it? You'll have to ask someone in Honesdale.

Downtown Honesdale has an extensive block of well-maintained century-old buildings.

Broadway, in Jim Thorpe, is the focal point for much of the tourist trade.

Kane is about the last place you would expect to see a temperature like this, but, whether or not the bank sign is accurate, it's hot!

Lake City, western Erie County … Some of the best sunsets you'll see anywhere are over Lake Erie.

In this Lewisburg scene, the building on the right was a stop on the Underground Railroad.

Third Street, Lewisburg, is loaded with stately old homes and towering church spires.

Lewistown, Mifflin County, has a great way to preserve knowledge about its downtown architecture.

In Ligonier and the surrounding area, you'll be aware of the French & Indian War connections.

Lititz Springs Park is one of the community's outstanding assets. *Budget Travel* magazine named Lititz as the 2013 coolest small town in America!

This old Reading Railroad caboose is found in Lititz Springs Park.

Downtown Lock Haven is — historic!

Looking across the Tioga River, you'll see Mansfield High School, and beyond that, Mansfield University.

Here and there, you'll find barber shops that have something extra, like this one in Mars.

The domes of St. Michael's Byzantine Catholic Church, in McAdoo, Schuylkill County, stand out in the evening sky.

A. Stoner. I honestly thought this was a put-on, but it isn't. It's a very appealing building in McConnellsburg, Fulton County.

Tim Hortons restaurants are so numerous in some parts of Canada, that it might be cheaper for provincial highway departments to install signs at exits where there is *not* a Tim Hortons! If you see one in Pennsylvania, you're most likely in the northwest, such as here in Meadville.

The Pike County community was home to Gifford Pinchot, twice governor, and the first head of the U.S. Forest Service.

Milford, along the Delaware River, boasts the superb Hotel Fauchère.

Wiconisco Creek, in Millersburg, just before it joins the Susquehanna. The footbridge was damaged by the September 2011 flood, but has since been re-opened.

Mount Joy was named by Scots-Irish settlers in honor of the *Mountjoy*, a ship that rescued the citizens of Londonderry, Northern Ireland, from starvation.

Eye-catching architecture like this is all over New Oxford, Adams County.

This fine building occupies a prominent position on New Oxford's town square.

"Newtown Hardware House" has a nice ring to it.

This elegant fountain graces downtown North East.

This may be "just a clock" in Orwigsburg, Schuylkill County, but it's an impressive one.

Morning fog over the Allegheny River provides the backdrop here in Oil City.

The building on the left, built in 1880, still evokes an earlier time in Oxford.

This small park in Quakertown separates east and westbound traffic.

Lake Raystown, located near Huntingdon, looks like it's been there forever, but it's the result of a dam that was completed in the 1970s.

Rain does not deter visitors to the annual Street Fair in downtown Selinsgrove, Snyder County.

There is no "SUV Day" in Selinsgrove, but maybe there should be!

Maggie Lemons, Nisha Orren, and Jenna Kapsar hold the last of their rapidly-melting banana splits here at the Selinsgrove Commons. Selinsgrove still holds the record for building the world's longest banana split (over four miles) back in 1988.

Stroudsburg is busy most of the time, but is even more so during the Pocono Raceway Festival.

Downtown in Ridgway, the bustling county seat of Elk County.

Right: Cameron Park, in Sunbury, separates east and westbound traffic on Market Street. Below: The Sunbury riverfront has undergone major redevelopment. Here, spectators gather to watch the "Cardboard Boat Regatta."

Built in a narrow valley, Tamaqua has several sets of steps to make it easier to get around.

If you know how busy it usually is in downtown Towanda, you could almost guess (correctly) that this was on a Sunday afternoon . . .

. . . but on a typical weekday, you'll find merchandise along the sidewalk in this Bradford County town.

US 6, which connects Bishop, California and Provincetown, Massachusetts, runs right through Troy.

This fine old building in Tyrone is not a fine old building at all! It's really two brick fronts, designed to look like it's a single structure.

Not one of those windows is real. This lady has had her eye on that plant for years!

Pride of place in Coudersport …

… and also pride in history.

Stephen G. Sheetz

Chairman of the Board, Sheetz, Inc.

Can you really talk about "small town" Pennsylvania without mentioning a Sheetz location? Although they also have locations in Ohio, West Virginia, Maryland, Virginia, North Carolina, and Florida, the Altoona-based company is nearly ubiquitous in western Pennsylvania and rapidly growing in eastern Pennsylvania. In some places, Sheetz is the biggest deal in town!

According to the Sheetz website, the company's modern origins date back to 1952, when Bob Sheetz purchased one of his father's five dairy stores. Brother Steve officially joined the company in 1969, and by 1983, they had opened their 100th store. Now, with over 450 stores in seven states, including more than 220 in Pennsylvania, the family-owned business continues to expand at the rate of about thirty-four stores a year, including eight to ten in the Keystone State.

What exactly do you call one of their stores? Steve Sheetz says that in the near future "Sheetz Convenience Restaurant" will be a common description. Steve believes the company owes its success to "fast, friendly service in clean, convenient locations." I'll add that MTOs (Made To Order food) are one of Sheetz's most appealing attractions. In addition, Sheetz is consistently rated as one of the best places to work in Pennsylvania.

Steve Sheetz in his office at company headquarters in Altoona.

Brittany Musselman and Ed Donnelly enjoy some coffee at, where else? — the Bloomsburg Sheetz!

A view from Council Cup Overlook, near Wapwallopen, looking north towards Shickshinny and Mocanaqua. Although there are many spectacular views throughout the state, this one gives me the opportunity to put Wapwallopen, Shickshinny, and Mocanaqua in the same sentence.

A merganser, followed by a merganserling (actually a duckling), is spotted in Warren.

A bird of another feather adds some color to a gray winter day in Warren.

The "Green" in Wellsboro lives up to its name, with the Tioga County Courthouse in the background.

The sculpture of Wynken, Blynken, and Nod can be found on the green. Nod is somewhere in the back, I think.

This tattoo parlor in Wrightsville, York County, has an interesting exterior. I'll leave the tattooing to the people who work there!

Even in winter, the canopy of elm trees graces Luzerne Street in Westmont.

Little Wyalusing, in Bradford County, has the equivalent of a "flatiron" building.

Galeton — small town, BIG fireworks!

Chapter Five:
Celebration and Remembrance

Too often, we really forget that some holidays are intended to allow us to pause and reflect about not only our own lives, but the lives of those who came before us and who, in so many cases, sacrificed so much, to make it possible for us to live in a better world. When November came around, I always asked my students if they knew why Veteran's Day is on November 11th and very few ever did. I suspect it's the same with adults as well. (The Armistice to end World War I was signed on November 11, 1918. We still live with some of the consequences of that war to this day.) Consider, in this next set of pictures, what we have to celebrate and what we have to remember.

A store window in Jim Thorpe reminds passersby of the Irish celebration.

Girardville, in Schuylkill County, puts on a big-time St. Patrick's Day parade.

In Conshohocken, St. Patrick's Day celebrations are big enough to close off Fayette Street.

Memorial Day ceremonies in Mercer are elaborate.

Veterans, of course, are given a prominent role in the day's proceedings.

The parade passes the courthouse.

In Waynesboro, the Fourth of July festivities attract residents of Franklin County, Pennsylvania, Washington County, Maryland, and beyond.

Marching down Main Street, past the historic Wayne Building.

Here come the Red Hatters!

Jersey Shore sets off quite a variety of fireworks from its school district's athletic fields … The colors of the Jersey Shore High School Bulldogs are orange and black. Here they are below — the colors, that is.

At the confluence of French Creek and the Allegheny River, Fourth of July fireworks in Franklin are unforgettable … They light up the river valley.

If this scene along the Susquehanna in Millersburg looks a little surreal, it's because it's a time exposure that makes it look somewhat lighter than it really was. An added bonus: that little white speck above the radio tower on the right is a shooting star!

In the wondrous setting of Potter County, tiny Galeton will give you an Independence Day fireworks show that seems to reach to the stars. An impatient spectator sets off his own pyrotechnics at the far end of the lake.

The Galeton celebration begins near the lake's shoreline.

Does anyone else see that partly hidden face at the top?

The scene over the Susquehanna is an inspiring sight. . .

. . . and the fireworks go on for a long time.

Not to overuse the word "spectacular," but the Galeton show *is* spectacular!

Nearly every community across the state has some sort of monument or memorial to commemorate a group of people or a special event. Think about that. If, instead of just glancing at one of them, you read and reflect on what each one says, you'll come away with a much greater appreciation for what all of them represent.

A thought-provoking tribute in Mt. Pleasant, Westmoreland County.

Part of a larger monument to all veterans in Renovo, Clinton County.

A memorial to all veterans in Mansfield.

This flag proudly flies over the Ohio and Beaver Rivers in Rochester.

More of the Renovo memorial, and this still isn't all of it.

City Park in DuBois.

The partially completed memorial to Flight 93 is in Somerset County.

At nearby Shanksville-Stonycreek High School are these inspiring words from Todd Beamer, a passenger on Flight 93.

Another monument to all veterans in Wellsboro.

Alongside the Fulton County Courthouse in McConnellsburg.

Multiple tributes can be found in a park in Carbondale, Lackawanna County ...

... including this one to Christopher Columbus.

A World War I monument in New Brighton, Beaver County.

You won't see too many of these: A monument to the Spanish-American War. This is located in Danville.

A memorial to Vietnam Veterans in Beaver.

In Athens, for the glory of country.

In Beaver, this is one of the larger Civil War monuments ...

... Beaver also has a monument remembering the Korean Conflict.

Said to be the only statue of George Washington in a British uniform, this is located in Waterford, Erie County. Still a British subject, Washington was in the area to tell the French it was "time to say *au revoir*."

North East honors its veterans in this downtown park.

In Driftwood, Cameron County, this monument recognizes the contributions of the Bucktail Regiment, a group of several hundred from the region who fought with distinction in the Civil War.

We're too far removed from the Civil War to appreciate how terrible it really was. The sheer number of Civil War monuments in Pennsylvania alone is remarkable. This one is in Montrose.

Part of a group of tributes in Monongahela, Washington County, this plaque recognizes those who are sometimes forgotten.

This plaque re-creates the famous picture taken at Iwo Jima during World War II.

We must have at least one tank, like this one in Brockway, Jefferson County.

Although this figure can be found in any number of places, the setting in Mansfield is especially inspiring.

Edinboro University, Erie County.

Chapter Six:

Campus Life

Actually, I didn't catch some of these places when there was much "life" going on, but my goal here was to show the variety of settings in which you'll find Pennsylvania's colleges and universities. Many of the most prestigious and accomplished institutions of higher learning anywhere in the U. S. are found right here in the Keystone State, and that includes some of the lesser-known ones. The following represents a completely arbitrary sampling, and makes no pretense of being comprehensive.

Few students are around on a brisk January day at Bloomsburg University …

… On the other hand, an exceptionally warm day in April brings them out by the hundreds!

A scene from Bucknell University, Lewisburg.

A sunny February day at Bucknell.

A westward-looking view from the heart of the California University campus.

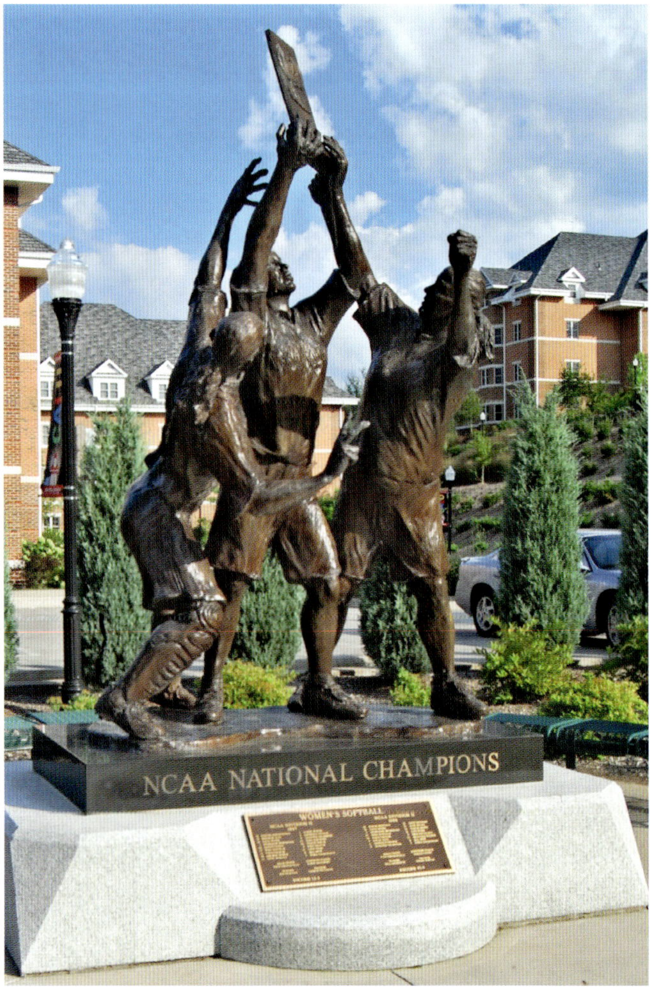

A tribute to the women's softball national championship team at California University in Washington County.

Cheyney University, in Delaware County, is the oldest historically black university in the country.

The "Fighting Scot" at Edinboro was dedicated in 2010.

These students, from New York City and Philadelphia respectively, told me that they love the relaxed pace at East Stroudsburg.

Pennsylvania Hall, the oldest building on the campus of Gettysburg College.

The Hall Building, on the campus of Haverford College, houses science classrooms.

If visitors to Gettysburg don't also stop to see Gettysburg College, they're missing a historic and stately campus.

This is farm country, so you might see the occasional tractor at Kutztown University.

… while a steady stream of band campers, or something, were coming through the campus, never more than a few at a time, so I finally took this shot as you see it.

This is not the Liberty Bell, but it is on the campus of Mansfield University …

Jesse Warner and Casey Leo enjoy a spring afternoon on the Kutztown campus …

… Mansfield University's North Hall, fronted by a timely reminder.

This Bald Eagle sculpture stands proudly on the campus of Lock Haven University …

… Winter on campus is invigorating, not depressing!

… One of the newer buildings on campus is the Durrwachter Conference Center.

On the campus of Marywood University, the Shields Center for Visual Arts is a piece of visual art in itself. The Marywood campus is partly in Scranton and partly in Dunmore.

The campus of Mount Aloysius College occupies a prominent position at the west end of Cresson in Cambria County.

Most of Penn State's branch campuses are located in larger towns, but PSU-Altoona is in a section called Ivyside — and you don't get any sense here that a big town is just down the road.

I noticed something interesting at PSU-Altoona. The lion shrine didn't seem to match my memory of the one on the main campus, shown here in a shot taken during the 1.7 seconds or so that people weren't having their pictures taken there. The ones on the branch campuses are identical to one another, but not to the main one (see below).

If this one looks *really different*, that's because it's a Pittsburgh Panther! This feline, on the campus of UP-Johnstown, doesn't look like the one on Forbes Avenue in Pittsburgh, either.

See for yourself at the PSU-Hazleton campus. This "alterna-cat" might have an ancestor in common with the one at the main campus. Maybe.

On the campus of St. Francis University, in Loretto, Cambria County, is this sculpture of "St. Francis and the Birds." The fountain is a replica of one in Assisi, Italy.

Roth Hall, the main administration building at Thiel College, in Greenville, Mercer County.

This is obviously a computer enhanced photo, but it's a real place. A more accurate rendering is on page 124.

Chapter Seven:

Signs

Don't Think Too Hard About Some of These!

Fishing Creek Creek, Speed Limit 11.5, Village of Panic? I believe that it was Witchcraft Road that inspired me to do this section, and I didn't have to go too far out of the way to find most of these. They just pop up here and there. Some of them really do make you wonder how they were named, and what I have found to be most amazing is how often local residents not only don't question a particular sign's origin, sometimes they don't think there is anything unusual about it!

The sign is correct. Bloomsburg *is* the only legally incorporated "town" in Pennsylvania.

While the official name of this municipality north of Pittsburgh is "Town of McCandless," its form of government isn't the same as that specified for a "town" according to the Pennsylvania code.

It would seem that there's a conflict here, but Bloomsburg's claim is solid. It is the only incorporated town in Pennsylvania. Why is Bloomsburg the only actual "town"? In the 1800s, organizing as a borough would have left part of Bloom Township too sparsely populated to be self-sustaining, so a local state senator engineered the passage of a special act of the legislature to create a town form of government. The main difference in this arrangement is that, unlike in a borough, the mayor is a voting member of council and presides over council meetings.

Ligonier is a borough, but community leaders can call their stately municipal building anything they want to!

The British and French couldn't agree on much of anything back in the day, not even on how to spell words whose origins didn't come from either language, hence the various spellings of this Native American-derived word.

Apparently, some people just can't get enough confusion in their lives.

The signs on the grounds of the Guthrie Clinic, in Sayre, are designed to get the attention of impatient drivers. Sometimes they even work.

The only sign I saw that identified Stalker, Pennsylvania (named for early settlers) was in Sullivan County, New York!

It may be the teacher in me, but every time I've seen this sign, near Breezewood, Bedford County, I've pictured the curves having to spend time in ISS (In School Suspension), you know, for being "bad."

You might as well make up your own story to explain how this town got its name. The four different versions that I read or was told about were unconvincing.

Another family name. No one seemed downtrodden. (A sixth grader could write a better caption!)

It's the names in these pictures, not the fire departments. They are both located in Cambria Township, just west of Ebensburg … If you just go "back and forth" with the two names a few times, you might see the connection.

I loved this sign the first time I saw it in Ambler, Montgomery County. It does get drivers' attention.

This one looks familiar. Like *in the previous picture* familiar! Someone in Tyrone had connections "back east," or so I was told. They're a bit more severe in Tyrone. The fine has been raised to $112!

What a great address! This is near Unionville, Chester County.

The modern day use of this word has negative connotations, but it refers to a Jewish group who fiercely fought against Roman rule in Palestine. This sign was "discovered" while coming to a complete stop in Wiconisco, Dauphin County.

We all get accustomed to something that others might consider unusual. Can there be very many "Zero" Streets in the world? This one is in Heidelberg, Allegheny County, and even town historians aren't sure of the origin of its name. There is a First Street (but, to be consistent, shouldn't it be "One" Street?).

It's in Windsor Township, Berks County, near Hamburg. Arising from traditional Pennsylvania Dutch folklore, this sign definitely will get your attention!

A Pittsburg without the "h," and in Pennsylvania, yet? Around 1890, an agency appointed by President Benjamin Harrison decreed that the final "h" would be dropped from place names ending in "burgh." After about twenty years of that, Pittsburgh (the big one) decided "no deal," so they were granted permission to reclaim the "h."

West Pittsburg apparently didn't think the issue was important enough, so the "h" remains absent. On the other hand, East Pittsburgh followed the lead of its much larger namesake.

West Pittsburg, spelled without the "h," is located about forty-five miles (more north than west) and two counties away from Pittsburgh.

Quite a hike from West Pittsburg is East Pittsburgh, nestled in a valley traversed by the George Westinghouse Bridge (pictured on the sign) and located much closer to the Steel City.

Trouble Ahead! Freeland and Eagles Mere, though some distance apart, are actually in neighboring counties. Clearly, however, there isn't much communication between the two, because something is wrong here!

The observant reader can work this one out, with the assistance of the good citizens of Freeland, Eagles Mere, Laporte, Mt. Jewett, Central City, Berlin, Somerset, and maybe a dozen or more other places in Pennsylvania.

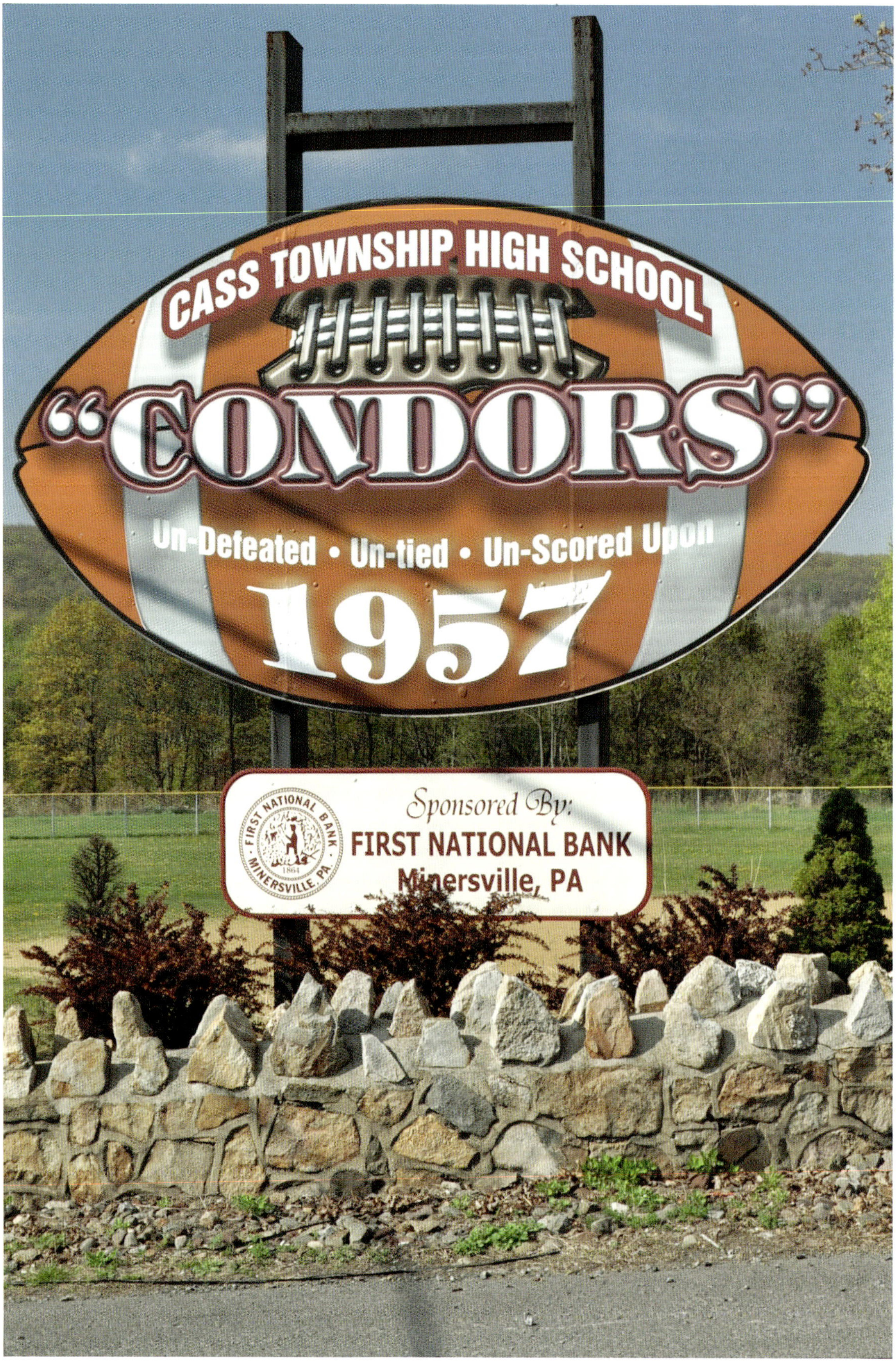

Located in Primrose, Schuylkill County, tiny Cass Township High School fielded a football team that accomplished what you see on this commemorative sign.

Chapter Eight:
Friday Night Lights

Plus some Saturdays and a Couple of Sundays

Granted, football is not for everyone, but there is no denying that, whether it's at the high school, college, or professional level, a substantial number of Pennsylvanians enthusiastically embrace the sport. The following photos attempt to show some of the scenes that go along with the typical autumn football day or night in Pennsylvania, from the comfortably warm days, right into the bitterly cold ones.

The sign at the "Silver Bowl" changes with every win.

Not far from Primrose, just over the line in Northumberland County, the Mt. Carmel Area Red Tornadoes had achieved their 813th win, more than any other Pennsylvania high school football team, by the end of the 2012 season.

Matt Cook, record-setting running back at Delaware Valley College, talks with Bill Scott, his high school coach at Selinsgrove, after a win at Lebanon Valley.

At Bloomsburg University, Dennis Iezzi, former assistant football coach at Kutztown University, has a post-game chat with one of his former players from Exeter High School.

George Curry has amassed over four hundred high school football wins, most of them at Berwick. He coached at Wyoming Valley West for a few years, but is once again a Bulldog, warming up for a game against Tunkhannock.

Amos Alonzo Stagg was one of the great pioneers in college football. Stagg Jr. and Sr. shared coaching duties at Susquehanna University in the 1950s and are honored on campus with this sculpture.

Andrea Bower and Steph Conklin are in the spirit as their Columbia Montour Vo-Tech Rams take on the East Juniata Tigers in Beaver Springs, Snyder County.

Cheerleaders at Penn-Trafford High School, in Westmoreland County, ring the bell for a touchdown scored by the Warriors against Greater Latrobe.

The student section arrives before most of the rest of the fans on this crisp October night.

"Dee-fence" is the word, in support of the Dynamos, in Springdale, Allegheny County.

Wilson High School Cheerleaders rev up the crowd as their Warriors take on the Bangor Slaters in this late November playoff game.

Alexa Moore goes high above the rest of her teammates to cheer on the Jersey Shore Bulldogs.

Taylor Bumbarger decided she could compete with the Curwensville Golden Tide, and became their very successful kicker.

At the District 9 championship game against Port Allegany, played in Brockway, the injured Shae Best wears his lucky beach towel. It worked — the Golden Tide won!

Members of the Towanda Black Knights wait for their turn to go face-to-face with the visitors from Wellsboro.

The Trinity Shamrocks meet the Middletown Blue Raiders for Middletown's homecoming, hence the "M" topped by a shamrock.

Devante King and Jay Hardenber, fresh from a muddy victory by Columbia Montour Vo-Tech over Nativity BVM of Pottsville.

A crisp November afternoon at Bucknell's Christy Mathewson stadium turned into . . .

. . . a bitterly cold day, when only a few diehards were still around to witness Bucknell's stunning overtime comeback win against Fordham.

Fans gather at the entrance for a nighttime game at Geneva College in Beaver Falls.

As the Clarion band energizes the crowd, the California Vulcans visit the Clarion Golden Eagles for Clarion's homecoming.

St. Thomas More, of Kentucky, visits the pristine campus of Grove City — and wins!

In this unusual, one time pairing of aquatic mammals, the host Selinsgrove Seals hang on to defeat the DuBois Beavers, at Harold L. Bolig Memorial Field, in Selinsgrove. Side note: As a member of the visiting Trenton Giants, then minor leaguer Willy Mays long-ago played under these very light standards, when they stood at Sunbury's minor league baseball field. (Talk about stretching trivia to a new limit!)

The "Pit" in Clarks Summit, Lackawanna County, is the scene of this rare Sunday afternoon game between the home team, Abington Heights, and the visiting Wyoming Valley West Spartans.

Members of the Selinsgrove Seals are warmly greeted at the high school parking lot on December 19, 2009, the morning after their state championship win in Hershey. Although the picture is becoming somewhat dated, the author is invoking "artistic privilege" to honor his hometown team!

For a great view, visit Redman Stadium, on the campus of Bloomsburg University. You'll probably see a great game, too!

The last rays of sunlight filter down to the Thomas Jefferson High School stadium in Jefferson Hills, Allegheny County. The TJ Jaguars have won three state AAA football titles.

Billing itself as "America's Largest Free Admission Amusement Park," Knoebel's Amusement Resort (or just "Knoebels" — the "K" is pronounced) has provided great entertainment for generations. The park, one of the most appealing you'll find anywhere, is located between Catawissa and Elysburg, in Columbia and Northumberland Counties.

Chapter Nine:

On the Midway and On the Street

Who doesn't like the atmosphere of an amusement park or a county fair? The smell of french fries or funnel cakes and the sounds of happy people (well, maybe the occasional whining of a cranky child) and the shrieks of people enjoying the dizzying rides all make you wonder why summer ever needs to end!

At the Jamestown Community Fair, in Mercer County, this display garnered a first-place award.

Evidently, it really is true about goats, like this one at the Centre County Grange Fair in Centre Hall. The wood doesn't look like it would be that tasty.

Other than to note that this is at the Greene County Fair, in Waynesburg, some pictures just don't need captions.

The sun still has a bit of light left for this day in Waynesburg.

The Bloomsburg Fair is one of the largest in the state.

In Bloomsburg, Derek Bankes gently tends to one of his sheep before an exhibition.

At the Elizabethtown Fair, this young man is giving the slide just a bit of thought ... while other fair-goers in "Etown" enjoy climbing vertical obstacles.

At the Carbon County Fair, in Palmerton, it would be unthinkable not to try some pierogies.

Pleasant summer night and a full moon — the perfect fair environment at the Clearfield County Fair.

Mike Krolikowski and Ralph Cragle take a break from working at the Clearfield County Fair to try their luck at one of the games. Working at Denny and Pearl's, owned by Mike's grandparents, is an all-summer long adventure throughout western Pennsylvania.

The owner of the cheerful smile is Veronica Krolikowski, Mike's sister. She also works for her grandparents during the summer and, in near one hundred-degree heat at the Big Butler Fair, took a break for this picture. As for the multicultural amphibian next to her, how would you fit that prize in your car? (Answer: Easy! Practically everyone drove a pick-up truck to get here!)

The Big Butler Fair is big, wonderful, and goes on for nine days.

Brady T. Wegener

Performer Extraordinaire

Billing himself as "The Class Clown," Brady Wegener, from Brackenridge, Allegheny County, has, in just a few years, learned how to become a first-class performer. Not only is he incredibly skilled, he knows how to entertain the crowd while he's multi-tasking juggling, balancing, vaulting, standing, sitting, and doing otherwise ridiculously difficult tricks. He engages in constant back and forth with the audience, and feeds off their "oohs" and "ahs." Mostly self-taught, he learned the basic mechanics in about a week. He has performed at numerous street fairs, but also some big regional events, including in New Jersey and Virginia.

I caught up with him in Butler, and when I asked him when he started juggling, I expected to get an answer like "age six," but, instead, he told me that he only began this when he was fourteen! On this rainy day, he was somewhat limited in what he could do for the camera, so what you see here doesn't adequately depict what he's capable of. It's still mighty impressive. You can catch some of his performances on YouTube.

Brady halts his frantic pace for this photo.

Along with performing the other action you see here, he's going from a standing to a sitting position. His skills are incredible!

Casey Gribble, along with Preston and Addison Snyder, work in the Snyder family business, at the Bellefonte Car Cruise.

DelGrosso's in Tipton, near Tyrone, might be as picture-perfect an amusement park as you'll find anywhere.

Of course DelGrosso's has its dizzying rides, which are for other people, not me.

She'll be on the big coasters before you know it!

The go-kart track is one of the big attractions here, but the nearby water slides and large pool are even bigger attractions.

Sometimes it's the sky that makes a picture, like this one at the Indiana County Fair.

At the Bedford County Fair, being the diversion for the serious bull riders is serious enough …

… Just ask either the bull, or the object of the bull's wrath! (Since, as English speakers, we read from left to right, I reversed the images on these two pictures, just in case you didn't notice.)

It may not appear to be the case, but Josiah is having the time of his life. This little guy may have set a record for speed around this track at Knoebels.

The 110-foot-high Ferris Wheel at Knoebels will give you a view of most of the park…

… but on the Twister, that same ferris wheel looks rather small. (It's between the right hand of Jenna Elmes, and the left hand of Justin Kressler.) This was the *last* chance I had to get a photo. The Twister is a great ride, especially if you're not carrying a two-pound camera around your neck!

Old-fashioned in some ways (all good), Knoebels still has a brass ring, or some kind of ring, to be snatched by the passing rider.

Sarah Shultz and Kaitlyn Raup enjoy their train ride through a tunnel, into the woods, and under a roller coaster.

Billy LeFevre and Jillian Christiansen motor their way through the course. The cupola in the background is a replica of one that once sat atop a factory in Shamokin.

On his day off from actually working at Knoebels, Alex Witcoskie came in just to get his picture in this book!

In Port Allegany, and anywhere else, if you have the skills, you'll be able to entertain fascinated onlookers with ease.

The sun is about to set at a long-time traditional fair in Gratz, Dauphin County.

Kennywood Park, in West Mifflin, south of Pittsburgh, is loaded with thrilling and stomach-churning roller coasters.

It also has a great old-time Midway.

One of the park's newer areas is graced by this collection of fountains.

A classy door, made even better for Christmas.

Chapter Ten:

Celebrating Christmas

At Christmas time, there's a feeling in the air that is unlike any other time of the year. This look at scenes related to Christmas is not intended to be exclusionary — only to recognize that the lines "city sidewalks, busy sidewalks..." are about real places.

To give you an idea of the size of this Santa Claus near Philipsburg, the soldiers are about life-size.

A nativity scene in downtown Sayre.

A store window in Bellefonte shows its red and green, and don't forget the train!

Nutcrackers at the Omni Bedford Springs Resort and Spa are just a small part of the Christmas décor in the fabulous interior.

At Byers' Choice® in Chalfont, Bucks County, you can find numerous scenes like this one year-round.

The displays are outstanding and each of the figurines, prized by collectors, is handmade by the great people who work there.

Carolers are on display in a half-mile-long setting on Christmas Boulevard in Berwick.

This building in Sunbury was "gift-wrapped" for only one Christmas season, but it, and a few others, drew lots of favorable attention.

In nearby Northumberland, the King Street Park gazebo is perfectly decorated for the Christmas season.

Stroudsburg is decked out in holiday wreaths.

It's just a temporary location for this tree in Bellefonte.

Christmas at the Penn Wells Hotel in Wellsboro will take you back in time — and you'll like it!

Here at Fleming's Christmas Tree Farm in Indiana County, buying a Christmas tree can be an adventure.

Many family-owned businesses are found in Indiana County, the "Christmas Tree Capital of the World." In Brush Valley, Den Mytrysak and Decker enjoy a moment of rest on a very busy day.

The backlighting in this nativity scene made this particular display stand out in Grove City.

A large and brilliant nativity scene alongside PA 31, in downtown Mt. Pleasant.

An appropriate scene in Nazareth. (The one in Pennsylvania.)

Fairlady and Company is ready for Christmas in Punxsutawney. Note the tin ceiling.

The Wintergarden at PPG Place, in downtown Pittsburgh, displays Santa Claus-type scenes from all over the world. The combination of these scenes, plus a model railroad display in the center of this great space, makes this a destination in itself.

A festival of trees in Tionesta.

The city of Warren offers warm greetings.

This scene, in Lewisburg, makes you want to sing "Silent Night."

In Wellsboro, these are "old toys," apparently.

A store window in Kittanning puts the emphasis on the shiny stuff. . .

. . . while, along the Kittanning riverfront, a late evening sky offers its Christmas red for the occasion.

A Dickensian display in Ebensburg.

Here and there, you'll find a German Christmas Market, such as the big one in Bethlehem, but Mifflinburg does an excellent job with its own.

The large tree in Mercer stands out on the courthouse lawn.

This display in Punxsutawney would be even better with snow …

… but the snow seems to be on the other side of the state, in Manheim, Lancaster County!

This mug, crafted by DiMartino Ice, of Jeannette, was one of the highlights at the Fire and Ice Festival in Lititz.

Chapter Eleven:
Ice (Solid H_2O) Sculptures

The biggest shame about ice sculptures is that they don't last. Many of them are true works of art and should probably be reproduced with glass made to look like ice. Remember, ice is just solid dihydrogen monoxide (water).

Steelers Country is not just in Ligonier, but practically everywhere in western Pennsylvania — and far beyond that.

The gazebo in Ligonier is the site for this DiMartino-created Elvis.

A backlit diamond in downtown Lewisburg.

A hot air balloon in Lititz.

Due to warm weather, this piece in Jim Thorpe is beginning to melt …

… But on Valentine's Day, this piece is still perfect.

When temperatures cooperate, ice carvings can hang on for some time. This one in Ebensburg is six days old!

Mid-January in Somerset is usually cold anyway, but, just in case somebody forgot that, here's a reminder that it's still winter.

Getting ready to do the carving in Franklin.

One of DiMartino's big projects at Franklin on Ice.

Jared McAlister, of DiMartino Ice, begins the carving in the Venango County town's February event. . .

. . . In Ligonier, Jared fine-tunes the shape of the crescent moon . . .

. . . while James Kowalczyk fire-polishes the finished product to give it its crystal like luster.

A fascinated onlooker watches James at work in Franklin.

The clarity of amber-colored maple syrup stands out at the Williams Family Maple Products facility in Saegertown, Crawford County.

Chapter Twelve:
Maple Syrup Weekends

Forget Vermont! Maple syrup is big business in Pennsylvania, too, and throughout late winter and early spring, you can enjoy a maple syrup weekend somewhere in the state. Lots of free samples!

The Howles family, near Blooming Valley, also in Crawford County, participates in the annual Maple Weekend in northwestern Pennsylvania.

Travis Howles demonstrates part of the process of making maple syrup (like, keeping the fire going).

Another step in making the sweet stuff is on display in Meyersdale, Somerset County.

In Meyersdale, this scene preserves days gone by.

Rhianna Browell is not hurting this tree! It's just a stump, for demonstration purposes.

It's Maple syrup hand-out time at Parker Dam State Park in Clearfield County.

In days of old, this yoke, shown at Hills Creek State Park in Tioga County, made it possible to carry two buckets of syrup at one time.

A late March snow blankets Raker's Sugar Bush in Liberty, Tioga County. Fred Moyer, along with family and friends from Snyder County, is here to sample the goods.

This display in Coudersport makes you want to sample everything.

A tapping demonstration at Fort Hunter, north of Harrisburg. Getting maple syrup out of this tree would be quite a feat, considering it's a black walnut!

Maple syrup is available in October, too, like here in Honesdale.

After seeing the window display at Patterson's Maple Farm, near Sabinsville, Tioga County, how could you resist a sample?

You make the best of a gray winter scene, like this one in Westmont, Cambria County.

Chapter Thirteen:
Life

"Life" ... now there's a clever title. This is intended to include a little bit of everything, so if the organization of this section seems somewhat unclear, well, that's life!

The combination of general store, railroad station, and post office offered advice on etiquette.

This was a big general store that served much of southeastern York County and part of Maryland.

Muddy Creek Forks, in York County, is just a spot in the road that makes you think you have stepped into the past.

The Easter egg hunt in Numidia, Columbia County, was over in a matter of seconds!

At the Sunbury River Festival, why allow something to be difficult when all you have to do is push this button?

A concert in downtown Hollidaysburg celebrates the Pumpkin Festival.

The threatening clouds went away without incident, and the show in Lewisburg went on as scheduled.

The legendary Ronnie Spector performs for a large and enthusiastic crowd at the John Murtha Amphitheater, on the banks of the Allegheny River, in Kittanning.

At their farm near Catawissa, Emily and Ron Dingle tend to their newborn goats. Emily's is only a week old while Ron's is only three days old!

Cute aren't they? They're wolf-dog hybrids, however, and they don't make good pets. When people discover that the hard way, it's fortunate that there is such a place as the Speedwell Forge Wolf Sanctuary in Lititz.

These are purebred wolves, and this particular group looks like they're sizing up Little Red Riding Hood. Once again: They do *not* make good pets!

Diane Sheddon rides "Bo" at the Troy Horse Show.

Allegedly a rat snake, at the Cross Fork Snake Hunt, in Potter County.

One of the many rescued animals at T & D's Cats of the World, in Penns Creek, Snyder County.

This is called a hooded grave. It's one of only two (there were three) in a tiny cemetery near Catawissa, Columbia County. There is some uncertainty as to their purpose, but supposedly, they were constructed either to ward off evil spirits or earthly grave robbers. Since the occupants have been unavailable for some time to offer any information, the reason for these structures may remain a mystery.

An old fire engine passes Shamokin's iconic Coney Island on Independence Street during the Anthracite Heritage Festival.

Mifflinburg commemorates "Buggy Days," not a reference to summertime pests, but to the buggy-making industry.

Waiting for the next customer is Amanda Jones, a very charming hostess at Muse, a restaurant in Oxford that features locally-grown products.

Little brother Arturo Linqui gets to be the punching bag for big brother Anthony Calderón in this scene from Berwick, but, hey, that's just the way life is!

It may look nostalgic, but this should be a reminder that the good old days, as re-created here at the Danville Iron Heritage Festival, could be rather grueling.

Eileen Garrison, of Pittsburgh, and Quang Dang, of Allentown, reunite at Hoffer Park in Middletown for this photo. Having had the privilege of being one of their high school teachers, I know that if there are enough people like these two out there, the country is in good, uh, hands.

Bruce and Lucy Henry demonstrate their dulcimer skills at the Laurel Festival in Wellsboro.

Melissa McHenry takes a break from the preliminary activities at the Benton Rodeo for this photo.

Anne F. Beiler

Entrepreneur and Motivational Speaker

The name might not be familiar, but the product almost certainly is. Anne and her husband, Jonas, are the founders of Auntie Anne's Pretzels, now located all over the United States, as well as internationally. Although the Beilers sold the company in 2005, Anne's life story is indelibly linked to that venture, and to her current endeavors.

It all started at the Downingtown Farmer's Market, in Downingtown Borough, Chester County, where, through trial and error, Anne and Jonas came up with just the right recipes. Neither of them believed that the company would ever become as big as it has, and, according to Anne, she thought that there might be "maybe fifty" locations someday. (It is now up to more than 1,200.) The sale of the company enabled Anne and Jonas to build The Family Center, a 55,000-square-foot community center in Gap, Lancaster County, that serves individuals mentally, spiritually, and physically. Additionally, according to Anne, the sale "allowed me to pursue my true passion, which is speaking to audiences and sharing my story. I love inspiring and motivating others to reach new levels in their own lives."

Asked how she would like people to think of her, Anne responded that she's been open with her life and willing to share "the good, the bad and the ugly," and is someone who cares for others and gives freely.

Anne Beiler takes a few minutes from her busy schedule at The Family Center in Gap, Lancaster County.

Courtesy of Auntie Anne's.

Chapter Fourteen:

Along the Way ... And Some That Got Away

Oftentimes, an unexpected scene or event captures your attention, practically demanding a picture be taken. It may be the composition, the lighting, or just a unique setting, but whatever the case, here they are: unplanned scenes that, for one reason or another, were attention-getters.

Along U. S. Route 6, just east of Corry, the skies had just started to clear in the west (to the right) as the sun was setting.

It isn't everyday that you see a structure this size being moved, as it is here in Willow Street, Lancaster County. As I remember, something else about this scene caught my attention, too.

I was going to resist using a picture of alpacas, but these gentle and curious creatures near Mt. Jewett, McKean County, were hard to ignore.

One night, walking in downtown Bellefonte, I thought this below street level window scene was interesting. Kind of gives you a warm feeling on a cold winter night, even if this picture was taken in July, and the place is now out of business.

After a particularly big snowfall in Red Hill, Montgomery County, workers at the local highway shed decided to make the best of the situation.

Is it the one from the east or the west who's wicked? I can never remember, but it really doesn't matter, since this one was flying out of the north, when she failed to consider the importance of this obstacle, near Wrightsville.

On the road to Damascus … well actually, this *is* Damascus. Just a country church in a remote section of Wayne County. If it looks like a piece of New England, well, why not? This part of Wayne County is closer to Pittsfield, Massachusetts than it is to Philadelphia, Pennsylvania!

West of Greencastle, in Franklin County, here's a combination of scene and sky, coming together just right for what, on another day, might have been nothing special.

A tribute to steel workers at the Edgar Thomson plant in Braddock.

At Skytop Lodge, near Canadensis, Monroe County, the accumulation of wintry mixes became overwhelming.

The last time I saw these bales of hay in Cashtown, Adams County, they were wearing their patriotic best. This time, it was for Easter.

Historians don't often treat him kindly, but James Buchanan will always be Mercersburg's native son.

The frequently-photographed barn near Cashtown is good enough for me, too.

It's just a country scene near Howard, Centre County.

A welcome center that's a tourist destination in itself. That's right, the Tioga Welcome Center, accessible only to US 15 southbound traffic coming into Pennsylvania from New York, is worth a trip to see the building — and the view of the Tioga River Valley below.

One of many highly interesting murals commemorating Lincoln Highway history, this one east of Chambersburg.

What caught my eye at this store near Stoneboro, Mercer County, was the state historical marker. It's a state marker, yes, but the state is California!

On a quiet residential street in Tamaqua is one of the most lovingly-cared for yards that you'll find anywhere. On numerous occasions during the year, the plant scheme is completely changed to reflect the time of year.

North of Greensburg, in Westmoreland County, you'll find this neatly painted repair shop.

Pronunciation Guide

Bala Cynwyd	BAL (rhymes with pal) – uh –KIN -wid
Conshohocken	CON – shuh – HOCK - in
Ebensburg	EBB – ins – burg
Emmaus	em – MAY – ess
Haverford	The "a" is short, as in "have"
Kinzua	KIN – zoo
Kutztown	Kutz rhymes with foots
Lackawanna	LACK – uh – WAHN – uh
Macungie	ma – CUN – jee
Mocanaqua	MOCK – uh – NOCK – wuh
Ohiopyle	Ohio + pile
Renovo	reh – NO – vuh
Schuylkill	SKOOLK – uhl
Selinsgrove	SEAL – ins – grove
(The middle syllable is INS, not INGS)	
Shamokin	sha – MO – kin
Shenandoah	SHEN – dough
(Not really, but that is how many local residents refer to it!)	
Shikellamy	SHIK – uh – LIMM – ee
Sinnemahoning	SINNA – muh – HONE – ing
Tamaqua	tuh – MOCK – wuh
Thiel	TEEL
Towanda	tuh – WAN – duh
Tunkhannock	tunk – HANN – uck
Wapwallopen	WOP – WALLA – pin
Wiconisco	WICK – uh – NIS – co
Wyalusing	WY – uh – LOOSE – ing
Youghiogheny	YOCK – uh – GAIN – ee
Zelienople	ZEEL – ee – uh – NO – puhl

Index

The Ones That Got Away

I had intended to include some pictures of post office murals, but due to some restrictions on their use by the U. S. Postal Service, it wasn't feasible to do so. I mention this not to be critical of the USPS, but to make readers aware of the existence of these works of art in post offices nationwide. They have their origins with the Works Progress Administration (WPA) of the 1930s, but became part of the Department of the Treasury's Section of Fine Arts. Photographs I had intended to include were from Athens, "General Sullivan at Tioga Point"; Bangor, "Slate Belt People," painted on four panels of slate; Canonsburg, "Beatty's Farm"; Catasauqua, "Arrival of the Stage"; and Mifflinburg, "Pioneers of the Community." These are truly artistic and historical treasures that everyone should be aware of. More information about them can be found at wpamurals.com.

And now, from Berwick's Christmas Boulevard, "That's All Folks"!